TAYLOR SWIFT

QUEEN OF REINVENTION

CARLA MOONEY

TWENTY-FIRST CENTURY BOOKS / MINNEAPOLIS

Twenty-First Century Books™
An imprint of Lerner Publishing Group, Inc.
241 First Avenue North
Minneapolis, MN 55401 USA

For reading levels and more information, look up this title at www.lernerbooks.com.

Main body text set in Gill Sans MT Std
Typeface provided by Monotype Typography.

Library of Congress Cataloging-in-Publication Data

Names: Mooney, Carla, 1970–author.
Title: Taylor Swift : queen of reinvention / Carla Mooney.
Description: Minneapolis : Twenty-First Century Books, 2025. | Series: Icons | Includes bibliographical references and index. | Audience: Ages 13–18 | Audience: Grades 7–9 | Summary: "Taylor Swift began her music career as a country singer. But over time she transitioned to pop and indie folk. Explore Swift's storied career, and how she continually reinvents herself while revolutionizing the music industry"—Provided by publisher.
Identifiers: LCCN 2024047641 (print) | LCCN 2024047642 (ebook) | ISBN 9798765670958 (library binding) | ISBN 9798765684917 (paperback) | ISBN 9798765682890 (epub)
Subjects: LCSH: Swift, Taylor, 1989-—Juvenile literature. | Singers—United States—Biography—Juvenile literature. | Country musicians—United States—Biography—Juvenile literature. | LCGFT: Biographies.
Classification: LCC ML3930.S989 M64 2025 (print) | LCC ML3930.S989 (ebook) | DDC 782.42164092 [B]—dc23/eng/20241008

LC record available at https://lccn.loc.gov/2024047641
LC ebook record available at https://lccn.loc.gov/2024047642

Manufactured in the United States of America
1 – CG – 7/15/25

CONTENTS

INTRODUCTION

WELCOME TO NEW YORK

On August 18, 2014, Taylor Swift waved from the top of the Empire State Building. With the city skyline in the background, Swift spoke directly to a live stream, saying, "Welcome to New York." Then the singer-songwriter walked into a studio filled with superfans. Swift quickly dropped a few surprises on her live audience and the fans watching the live stream around the world. First she played a new song, "Shake It Off." To the delight of her fans, Swift announced the song was part of a new album she had been working on for the past two years. Swift said the album was a "kind of rebirth" for her, and she titled it *1989* in a nod to the year she was born.

The album and its opening track, "Welcome to New York," paralleled Swift's life. Ten years into her career, Swift was poised to change her life and music significantly. She had recently left Nashville to settle into New York's trendy

Swift poses at the top of the Empire State Building in August 2014 as she prepares to announce a new album.

Tribeca neighborhood. "New York kind of pulled me here like a magnet. I was intimidated by the fact that it was bright and bold and loud. And now I know that I should run towards things like that," she said in a 2014 *Time* article.

Swift credited New York City with inspiring her songwriting for her new album. The city's excitement and endless possibilities pushed her to do something new with her music. Swift had been known as a country artist with some pop country songs up to this point. But *1989* was different. It was her first entirely pop album. With *1989* Swift refused to be limited in the type of music she made. She made it clear that she would express herself in a wide range of musical sounds and styles. For Swift fully embracing pop music in *1989* was a relief. "This album was made completely and solely on my terms, with no one else's opinion factoring in, no one else's agenda factoring in. I didn't feel that I was having to think too hard about the musical direction. In the past, I've always tried to make sure that I was maintaining a stronghold on two different genres, and this time, I just had to think about one, which was creatively a relief. It was nice to be honest about what I was making," Swift told *Billboard* in 2014.

"This album was made completely and solely on my terms . . ."

—Taylor Swift, 2014

1989 was not just another Taylor Swift album—it was a turning point in her career. The country twang that fueled Swift's early music was gone, replaced with an unapologetically pop sound. The album was a risk that Swift embraced. Her faith in herself paid off. *1989* was a phenomenal success in every way. The album hit number one on the *Billboard* chart and remained in the top ten for an entire year. *1989* was Swift's first album to have multiple number one hits on the *Billboard* Hot 100, including "Shake It Off," "Blank Space," and "Bad Blood" with Kendrick Lamar. At the 2018 Grammy Awards, Swift won three Grammys for *1989*, including her first Album of the Year award.

With *1989* Swift transformed from a country singer and songwriter to a pop music superstar. She did it by following her instincts and remaining authentic to herself. Swift's reinvention showed the world that she had become one of her generation's most influential musical voices.

1

Early Life and Musical Dreams

Taylor Swift began singing not long after she could talk. "She was always singing . . . when she was 3, 5, 6, 7, years old. It's Taylor doing what she likes to do," said her father, Scott Swift, in a 2009 interview with *UDaily* at the University of Delaware. At the time Taylor's parents, Scott and Andrea Swift, had no idea what the future held for their daughter.

Singing in Pennsylvania

Born on December 13, 1989, Taylor Alison Swift spent her early life on a former Christmas tree farm outside the small town of Reading, Pennsylvania. When Taylor was two years old, her parents welcomed a son named Austin. Her father, Scott, worked as a financial executive for an investment firm, while Andrea, her mother, was a former marketing executive focused on raising her two young children.

Taylor has always had a close bond with her parents, Scott and Andrea Swift, and has credited them with supporting her dreams from a young age and helping her find success throughout her career.

As a child Taylor had an active imagination. One of her favorite things to do was make up fairy tales and sing songs from Disney movies. At age six Taylor listened to music by country artist LeAnn Rimes and fell in love with the musical style.

Taylor joined a children's musical theater company to explore her interest in music. For her the highlight of the experience was not acting on stage but going to cast parties where there was a karaoke machine. She serenaded the parties with covers of popular country songs.

Taylor spent many happy years in her Pennsylvania childhood home. She credits the setting as being the perfect place for her to let her imagination run wild.

Local Performances

Taylor searched for more places to sing. At age eleven she discovered a weekly karaoke contest at the Pat Garrett Roadhouse in Strausstown, Pennsylvania. For more than a year, Taylor's parents drove her to the bar every week so that she could sing in the contest. Finally Taylor won with a cover of "Big Deal" by LeAnn Rimes. Her prize was being added as an opening act for country singer Charlie Daniels at a nearby amphitheater, though Taylor sang hours before Daniels took the stage.

Next Taylor began to sing the national anthem at local sporting events. In 2002 the twelve-year-old landed her biggest opportunity to date. After her father sent in an audition tape, she was picked to sing the national anthem before a Philadelphia 76ers basketball game. At Philadelphia's First Union Center, Taylor sang the anthem in front of more than twenty thousand people.

A Trip to Nashville

After watching biographies of country music stars, Taylor knew Nashville was the place to be. She convinced her mother to fly to Nashville's Music Row with a demo CD of her singing karaoke songs. Nashville's Music Row is home to many country record label offices, recording studios, and radio stations. With her mother and younger brother waiting in the car, young Taylor knocked on record labels' doors, introduced herself, and told everyone she met that she was looking for a record deal. No offers came.

The rejections lit a fire in Taylor. She realized that she needed to do more than sing karaoke songs. She needed to write her own songs and play the guitar to get noticed by the music industry. Taylor started taking guitar lessons from a local musician and computer tech named Ronnie Cremer. She played the guitar for hours daily, so much so that her fingers cracked and bled. Her mother would tape up Taylor's fingers, and she would keep playing. Cremer also helped Taylor with her songwriting. He showed her how to use songwriting software. Taylor took his lessons and wrote "Lucky You," her first song.

Middle School Challenges

While Taylor had no trouble singing in front of thousands of people, attending middle school was more of a challenge.

Faith Hill

Taylor Swift credits country star Faith Hill as an early mentor and influence on her music and career. Hill is one of country music's top artists, selling more than forty million albums worldwide. Hill also had crossover appeal, with several of her albums and songs achieving success on pop charts and earning Hill three Grammy awards.

Country superstars Faith Hill (*left*) and Tim McGraw (*right*) gave Swift valuable advice early in her career.

As a child Swift watched a television show about Faith Hill, which sparked her desire to go to Nashville. In 2007 Swift met Hill and her husband, Tim McGraw, at the Academy of Country Music Awards. When a teenage Swift opened for Tim McGraw's Soul2Soul Tour, she had long conversations with Hill and McGraw in Hill's dressing room and absorbed advice from the country couple. Later Swift talked about how Hill would reach out to her frequently, and the two built a relationship where Swift knew she could talk to Hill whenever she needed.

Many classmates thought that country music was uncool. They teased Taylor about her curly hair and left her to eat alone at lunch.

Taylor found comfort in music. "When I picked up the guitar, I could not stop. I would literally play until my fingers bled . . . and you can imagine how popular that made me: 'Look at her fingers, so weird,'" she said in *Rolling Stone* in 2009. "But for the first time, I could sit in class and those girls could say anything they wanted about me, because after school, I was going to go home and write a song about it."

Move to Nashville

After performing the national anthem at the US Open Tennis Championships in 2002, Taylor caught the eye of music manager Dan Dymtrow, who also managed music superstar Britney Spears. Dymtrow began working with Taylor and helped her land a modeling gig for Abercrombie & Fitch. One of her original songs was included in a Maybelline makeup promotional CD.

Dymtrow also arranged for Taylor to perform her original songs at an RCA Records showcase. This time music professionals noticed. At age thirteen Taylor signed an artist development deal with RCA. In the development deal, RCA committed to working with Taylor to develop her musical skills and artist profile. For the next year, Taylor and her mother traveled regularly to Nashville so she could work with the label.

Now that she was working with RCA, Taylor convinced her parents it was time to move to Nashville. In 2003 the Swift family moved to Hendersonville, a town outside of Nashville, and Scott transferred his office to Nashville. Scott

A teenage Taylor sparkles as she sings the national anthem in Philadelphia during a professional baseball game.

and Andrea wanted to help Taylor pursue her dream, but they firmly believed their daughter should not feel pressured into a music career.

Taylor had weekly, two-hour writing sessions in Nashville with several country songwriters, including Brett James, Troy Verges, the Warren Brothers, and Liz Rose. Even though she was only a freshman in high school, Taylor impressed Rose with her focus and dedication to her music. Rose later collaborated with Taylor on several songs, including her first hit, "Tim McGraw."

As Taylor worked hard at songwriting, RCA was more interested in her singing other songwriters' work. Taylor decided not to renew her development deal with the company. She felt strongly that her writing would set her apart from other country artists.

Big Machine Records

The decision proved to be the right one. In late 2004 Taylor was invited to play in a showcase at Nashville's Bluebird Café, where country legends Garth Brooks and Faith Hill had been discovered years earlier. Music executive Scott Borchetta was in the audience and immediately took notice of the young musician. Borchetta had just left his job with Universal Records and was starting his independent record label, Big Machine Records. After talking with Borchetta, Taylor signed with Big Machine Records in 2005.

With Borchetta Taylor began working on her debut album and recorded it in only four months. Her first single, "Tim McGraw," was released in June 2006. At the time Big Machine Records was still a new company with only ten employees. Taylor and Andrea stuffed envelopes with the CD to send to radio stations, often sitting on the floor because the label's office did not have furniture.

Andrea used her marketing skills to help Taylor promote her debut album. They embraced the social media site Myspace, where Taylor connected with fans and gathered feedback on songs. Taylor wrote her bio and blogs and personally responded to fan comments. Within a year Taylor's music hit fourteen million streams on the social media platform.

First Album: *Taylor Swift*

The self-titled album *Taylor Swift* released in October 2006. It featured hit singles "Tim McGraw," "Teardrops on My Guitar," and "Our Song." To promote the album, Taylor toured as an opening act for several country artists, including Brad Paisley, Rascal Flatts, George Strait, Tim McGraw, and Faith Hill.

The debut album was a commercial success, rising to the top of *Billboard*'s Top Country Albums and selling more than seven million copies. It was also nominated for several awards and won a Breakthrough Video of the Year Award for "Tim McGraw" at the 2007 Country Music Awards.

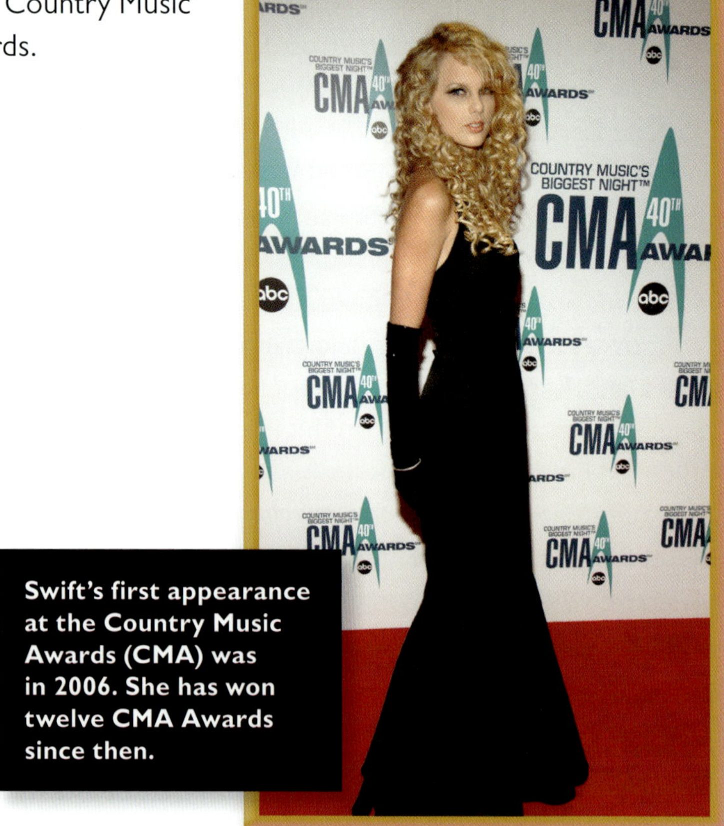

Swift's first appearance at the Country Music Awards (CMA) was in 2006. She has won twelve CMA Awards since then.

A Rise to Fame

After the success of her debut album *Taylor Swift*, some wondered if Swift could achieve similar success with her second album. Had the teenage country singer already reached her peak? Would she be able to navigate a lengthy career?

For a year after *Taylor Swift*'s release, Swift traveled the country as an opening act. The grueling tour schedule gave her a lot of time alone. She used the time to write more music, enough for a new album.

Fearless

Swift released her second album, *Fearless*, in November 2008. Everyone at the studio felt pressured to follow *Taylor Swift* with another hit. "There was definitely an unwritten stress," studio engineer Chad Carlson told *Rolling Stone*. "We knew we could make a monster record, but we put a lot of pressure in [sic] ourselves." Swift wrote seven of the album's songs without a cowriter. She also coproduced for the first time.

Swift celebrates backstage with four Grammys at the 2010 Grammy Awards. She won Album of the Year (*Fearless*), Best Country Album (*Fearless*), Best Country Song ("White Horse"), and Best Female Country Vocal Performance ("White Horse").

Fearless debuted at number one on *Billboard*'s Top Country Music Albums. With *Fearless* Swift established her mainstream appeal beyond country music. The album's first single, "Love Story," became a crossover hit and reached number four on the US *Billboard* Hot 100 chart. Four other hit singles were released from *Fearless*, including "White Horse," "You Belong With Me," "Fifteen," and "Fearless." *Fearless* became the top-selling album of 2009 in the United States and earned Swift her first Grammy award for Album of the Year.

Country and pop audiences connected with Swift's relatable lyrics on *Fearless*. "Two albums in, Taylor Swift is sounding less like a novelty act than like someone who already knows that a lot of us never stop experiencing those feelings of righteous anger, insecurity, and giddiness," music critic Ken Tucker said to NPR.

With her popularity soaring, Swift kicked off the *Fearless* Tour, her first headlining concert tour, in 2009. With 118 shows across the United States, Canada, Australia, and England, the tour grossed more than sixty-three million dollars. On stage Swift performed on theatrical sets with multiple costume changes, elements that would become staples of her future concerts.

Swift wears a marching band uniform while performing "You Belong With Me" during the 2009 *Fearless* Tour.

Swift won multiple awards for *Fearless*, including Artist of the Year at the American Music Awards and Album of the Year at the Country Music Awards. She won four Grammys in 2010, including Album of the Year and Best Country Album. *Billboard* named her the Artist of the Year in 2009.

Fearless established Swift as an artist with crossover appeal. Listeners embraced her earnest lyrics and singable melodies. The album solidified Swift's reputation as a talented songwriter and performer, forming a foundation for her future music.

Speak Now

By the time the *Fearless* Tour ended in 2010, Swift was ready to get into the studio to record her third album. The result was *Speak Now*, a highly personal album released in October 2010 by Big Machine Records. Swift had written each of the album's fourteen songs about experiences in her life over the past two years, from love to heartbreak. Swift described the album in an interview with *Songwriter Universe*. "In life, you have a lot of situations that pop up and people that come into your life, and sometimes you don't get to tell them what you wish you would have told them," Swift said. "This album is my opportunity to do that track-by-track. Each song is a different confession to a different person. Some of the things I wrote about are things everyone saw me go through," she added. "Some of the things I wrote about are things nobody ever knew about. I'm beyond excited for you to hear these stories and confessions," she said.

Speak Now was a testament to Swift's songwriting brilliance. In her lyrics she continued the bare honesty she had become known for while hinting at the storytelling she

Swift belts out a ballad during her *Speak Now* Tour.

would employ on future albums. Most importantly *Speak Now* announced that Taylor Swift was determined to speak her mind and never leave anything unsaid.

Speak Now was a smashing success and sold more than one million copies in its opening week in October 2010, nearly double what *Fearless* had sold in its first week. *Speak Now* became the fastest-selling new album in five years. It debuted at number one on the *Billboard* 200 chart. Fans hunted for clues on each song to figure out who Swift was talking to with her lyrics. For example many believed the song

“Mean” was directed at critic Bob Lefsetz, who had publicly criticized Swift’s performance with Stevie Nicks at the 2010 Grammy Awards. By the end of 2010, *Speak Now* had sold nearly three million copies, making it the third best-selling album of 2010. The album continued to sell for more than a decade, and by January 2024, *Speak Now* had sold 4.8 million copies in the United States.

Speak Now was nominated for several awards. It won the Top Country Album award at the *Billboard* Music Awards. At the 2012 Grammy Awards, *Speak Now’s* single “Mean” won Best Country Solo Performance and Best Country Song.

Red: A Breakup Album

By 2010 Swift’s fame had risen to a new level. Paparazzi followed her everywhere, hoping to catch a glimpse of Swift’s romantic life. They sold pictures to tabloid magazines that peddled rumors about her love life, boyfriends, and breakups. After her much-publicized breakup with actor Jake Gyllenhaal in 2012, Swift recorded her fourth studio album, *Red*.

On *Red* Taylor laid bare the feelings that came with her recent breakup. “I look back on [*Red*] as my true breakup album, every other album has flickers of different things. But this was an album that I wrote specifically about pure, absolute, to the core, heartbreak,” she told *Rolling Stone* in 2020. Several songs on *Red* spoke to the end of her relationship, including “We Are Never Ever Getting Back Together” and “All Too Well.”

For *Red* Swift worked with new producers and songwriters, including Ed Sheeran and Max Martin, as well as long-time collaborators Nathan Chapman and Liz Rose. The first single from *Red*, “We Are Never Ever Getting Back

"All Too Well"

On her *Red* album, Swift's song "All Too Well" is widely believed to be about her ex-boyfriend, actor Jake Gyllenhaal. Twenty-year-old Swift and twenty-nine-year-old Gyllenhaal dated for three months in 2010. Fans have found several clues that point to Gyllenhaal being the subject of "All Too Well." One hint was found in *Red*'s liner notes, which included a secret message for "All Too Well" that read "MAPLE LATTES." Fans believe this points to the couple's Thanksgiving date at a coffee shop where they drank maple lattes. The song's lyrics also mention a scarf left at the subject's sister's house, a nod to Swift's scarf that was reportedly left at Gyllenhaal's sister's house on Thanksgiving. On *Red (Taylor's Version)*, Swift released a ten-minute version of "All Too Well," which hinted at the couple's age difference as the reason for their eventual breakup.

Actor Jake Gyllenhaal is rumored to be the subject of several of Swift's songs. However, Gyllenhaal has remained silent about his past relationship with Swift.

Together," became Swift's first song to reach the top of the *Billboard* Hot 100 chart. It stayed on top for three weeks. Her third single from the album, "I Knew You Were Trouble," peaked at number two on the *Billboard* Hot 100.

With *Red* Swift continued to push the boundaries between country and pop music.

Red released in October 2012 and debuted at number one, making it Swift's third album to do so. The album sold a record-setting 1.2 million copies in its opening week. It became the second-highest-selling album of 2012, selling 3.11 million copies by December. As of January 2024, *Red* had sold 4.58 million copies. Swift promoted the album on the *Red* Tour, which ran from March 2013 to June 2014. The tour, which traveled to venues on four continents, grossed a record-breaking $150 million for a country tour.

Red was nominated for several awards, including Album of the Year and Best Country Album at the 2014 Grammy Awards. *Red* won Top Country Album at the 2013 American Music Awards. It also took home trophies at the *Billboard* Music Awards, including Top Album and Top Country Song for "We Are Never Ever Getting Back Together."

With *Red* Swift continued to push the boundaries between country and pop music. Before *Red* Swift experimented with a pop sound but did not stray far from her country roots. Now she was ready to take the leap.

3

Pop Stardom

In 2014 Taylor Swift made a career-defining decision. So far Swift's music had blended her country roots with a dose of pop sound. Now she deliberately chose to move entirely into the pop arena. Her fifth studio album, *1989*, solidified Swift as one of the most successful and influential pop artists of the time.

A Pop Connection

After the release of *Red* in 2012, Swift was one of the biggest artists in country music. *Red* paid tribute to her country roots, but it also expanded Swift's artistry to include a dance-pop sound. The songs on *Red* with a pop sound had two things in common: they were co-produced by Max Martin and Karl "Shellback" Schuster.

Martin and Schuster were established pop producers before working with Swift in 2012. Martin had written and coproduced hits such as "Baby One More Time" by Britney Spears and "So What" by Pink. Shellback had collaborated on

The original cover art for Swift's *1989* album features a Polaroid picture of the singer.

hits such as "Moves Like Jagger" by Maroon 5 and Usher's "DJ Got Us Fallin' In Love."

Swift explained the decision to work with Martin and Schuster again on *1989* in a *Billboard* interview. "Max Martin and Shellback were the last people I collaborated with on *Red*, and I wished we could have done more and explored more. So going into this album, I knew that I wanted to start with them again. Then I thought, 'Wouldn't it be amazing to work with Ryan Tedder?' And then I was with Jack Antonoff and Lena Dunham at the beach, and we started talking about our favorite '80s music. All of this started happening organically, and I found myself gravitating toward pop sensibilities, pop hooks, pop production styles," she said.

With Martin as co-executive producer, Swift created an album with a polished, pop sound that differed from her previous work. She broke the news to Scott Borchetta at Big

Machine Records and told him that her new work was not a country album. "He went into a state of semi-panic and went through all the stages of grief—the pleading, the denial. 'Can you give me three country songs? Can we put a fiddle on 'Shake It Off'?' And all my answers were a very firm 'no,' because it felt disingenuous to try to exploit two genres when your album falls in only one. I never want to pull the wool over people's eyes, because people are so much smarter than a lot of marketing professionals give them credit for," Swift said to *Billboard*.

Shaking Off the Past

The lead single "Shake It Off" was released in August 2014. The energetic, upbeat song with catchy lyrics was an instant hit. It debuted at number one on the *Billboard* Hot 100 and

Bad Blood

The song with the most bite on *1989* is "Bad Blood" with Kendrick Lamar. The song was rumored to be about pop artist Katy Perry. Although Swift never named Perry, she talked about an unnamed star who pretended to be her friend, but then allegedly tried to steal Swift's arena tour employees. "I was like, 'Oh, we're just straight-up enemies.' And it wasn't even about a guy! It had to do with business," Swift explained to *Rolling Stone*. With "Bad Blood," Swift had another number one hit song and a star-filled music video that won Swift's first MTV Video of the Year Award in 2015.

Swift poses with Kendrick Lamar. She collaborated with Lamar on *1989*'s highly successful track "Bad Blood."

spent four weeks at the top. Swift talked about the single and the message it sent to her fans. "That song is essentially written about an important lesson I learned that really changed how I live my life and how I look at my life. I really wanted it to be a song that made people want to get up and dance at a wedding reception from the first drum beat. But I also wanted it to be a song that could help someone get through something really terrible, if they wanted to focus on the emotional profile, on the lyrics," she said to *Billboard*. The "Shake It Off" music video featured Swift dancing awkwardly in various styles, showing she was comfortable poking fun at herself.

1989 hit stores in October 2014 and debuted at the top of the *Billboard* 200 chart. The album sold 1.28 million copies in the United States in its first week, becoming Swift's third consecutive album to do so. The album included thirteen songs, plenty of pop synthesizers, pulsating bass, and processed backing vocals. Unlike Swift's previous albums, an acoustic guitar could only be heard on one song. When writing and recording *1989*, Swift was inspired by some of her favorite 1980s pop artists, including Annie Lennox, Phil Collins, and Madonna.

1989 produced a series of hits that played across radio stations and climbed the charts. The album's second single, "Blank Space," was a sarcastic response to the media's portrayal of Swift as a serial dater. Critics praised the song's clever lyrics and satire, while fans boosted it to become another number one hit on the *Billboard* Hot 100. When "Blank Space" replaced "Shake It Off," Swift became the first woman to replace herself at the top of the chart.

Another hit single from *1989* was "Style," which was rumored to be inspired by Swift's relationship with pop star Harry Styles. Although Swift does not explicitly name whom she writes her songs about, she frequently hides clues in her album notes and makes cryptic comments that give subtle hints to her fans. The challenge to decipher her lyrics and uncover the clues Swift leaves makes each album release even more entertaining for her die-hard fans.

The transformation from country singer-songwriter to global pop superstar was a risk that paid off for Swift. *1989* won numerous awards, including the Grammy for Album of the Year in 2015. Swift became the first female artist to win this award twice. With *1989* Swift established herself as a leading figure in pop music. She showed that she could reinvent herself and her music while staying true to her identity as a storyteller.

The *1989* World Tour: A Global Phenomenon

The *1989* World Tour was a monumental event in Swift's career, further solidifying her global pop stardom. From May to December 2015, the tour visited four continents and became one of the highest-grossing tours of all time, generating over $250 million.

The tour featured elaborate staging, choreography, and special effects. At one point Swift danced on an enormous rotating platform while performing "Shake It Off." Throughout the tour fans were treated to several celebrity guest appearances, including Ellie Goulding, Justin Timberlake, Alanis Morissette, Mick Jagger, and Selena Gomez. In between songs Swift interacted with fans and shared personal stories, another regular feature of her live performances. The *1989* Tour became one of the pop culture events of the mid-2010s, and Swift solidified her position as one of the top live performers worldwide.

4

The Glare of Fame

After the success of *1989*, Swift's global fame skyrocketed. And with that fame came increasing scrutiny of her personal life, especially her relationships. From the beginning of her career, Swift had been an open book about relationships, pouring her feelings and experiences into the lyrics of her songs. Now, however, the attention on her life outside of the studio and stage intensified. Headlines trumpeted her latest romantic partners and followed her relationships with celebrities such as Harry Styles, Calvin Harris, and Tom Hiddleston. Swift found herself trying to navigate the pressure of the intense public attention.

Swift vs. Kanye

In 2016 a long-standing public feud between Swift and rapper Kanye West intensified. The conflict between the two artists began in 2009 at the MTV Video Music Awards when nineteen-year-old Swift won the Best Female Video award

Kanye West interrupts Swift on stage as she accepts an award at the 2009 MTV Video Music Awards.

for "You Belong With Me." As Swift was on stage giving her acceptance speech, West jumped on stage and grabbed the microphone from her and announced that Beyoncé should have won the award. Stunned, Swift left the stage. West was asked to leave the awards show, and when Beyoncé won Video of the Year later that night, she took the opportunity to bring Swift back on stage to finish her speech.

The feud simmered for several years but escalated in 2016 when West released a new song, "Famous." In the song West rapped derogatory lyrics about Swift, which hinted at a future relationship between the two artists and claimed that

West made Swift famous. While West claimed that he had gotten Swift's approval for the lyrics, Swift's team immediately released a statement denying that she knew about or approved the specific lyrics West used. Swift herself stayed silent on the controversy, but others in her circle spoke out in her defense. Her brother, Austin, posted a video on social media where he threw his Yeezy sneakers—a brand created by West—in the garbage.

The conflict grew hotter when West's then-wife, Kim Kardashian, claimed in an interview that Swift had approved West's lyrics and called Swift a snake on social media. To support her claim, Kardashian later released a secret recording of a phone call between West and Swift. The edited recording appeared to support West's claim that Swift had agreed to his lyrics. Swift insisted that she was not told the full content of the lyrics, and Kardashian's edited recording did not accurately reflect the conversation.

The damage was done. A widespread public backlash against Swift that had been building in recent months exploded. Online the hashtags #TaylorSwiftIsOverParty and #KimExposedTaylorParty began trending. Swift responded to the controversy by retreating from the public eye for much of 2016 and part of 2017. She handled her emotions over the controversy and backlash as she had done for much of her life: she wrote new music.

Reclaiming Her Narrative

In late 2017 after a year of public silence, Swift returned with her sixth studio album, *Reputation*. During her time out of the public eye, Swift channeled her experiences into the new music. The album's lead single, "Look What You Made Me

Swift talks with Kim Kardashian and Kanye West at the 2015 MTV Video Music Awards. The feud between the artists still simmered and would surface again in 2016.

Do," was released in August 2017. The song had a darker, edgier sound than much of Swift's previous work. The music video for the single featured Swift shedding her old character and embracing a new, darker image. Some of the song's lyrics hinted at the singer's feud with West and Kardashian, including:

> I don't like your little games
> Don't like your tilted stage
> The role you made me play
> Of the fool
> No, I don't like you

On the day of its release, the song and its video broke streaming records on YouTube and Spotify as the single rose to number one on the *Billboard* Hot 100 chart.

In November 2017 Swift released the full album. Although Swift never publicly confirmed the subject of her lyrics, several songs on *Reputation* appeared to be pointed at West and Kardashian. In "I Did Something Bad," the lyrics, "They're burning all the witches even if you aren't one / They got their pitchforks and proof / Their receipts and reasons," are believed to be about West and Kardashian. In "This Is Why We Can't Have Nice Things," Swift alludes to the secret

Swift performs during her record-breaking *Reputation* Stadium Tour. Artists Camila Cabello and Charli XCX were the opening acts on Swift's tour.

Vindication

In 2020 the full twenty-five-minute video recording of Swift and Kanye West's infamous 2016 phone call leaked online. Swift's fans, known as Swifties, immediately pounced and claimed that the complete video, without Kim Kardashian's heavily edited excerpts, proved that Swift had been telling the truth the entire time. The full recording showed Swift and West discussing West's "Famous" lyrics, but he never read Swift the line that she objected to and in particular, the derogatory word he used. Swifties took to social media, and soon a new hashtag began trending, #KanyeWestIsOverParty.

recorded phone call with the lyric: "It was so nice being friends again / There I was giving you a second chance / But you stabbed me in the back without shaking my hand."

Reputation was a critical and commercial success, though its tone was notably different from Swift's previous work. It became the biggest-selling album in the United States in a single week, selling 1.23 million copies. Swift chose to keep *Reputation* off streaming services such as Apple Music and Spotify for three weeks, so fans were forced to buy the album, which drove album sales.

In 2019 Swift talked to *Vogue* about how the conflict with West and Kardashian in 2016 changed her life. "A mass public shaming, with millions of people saying you are quote, unquote canceled, is a very isolating experience," she said. "I don't think there are that many people who can actually understand what it's like to have millions of people hate you

Swift's *Reputation* Tour featured an enormous snake on stage. Fans believe the snake was a nod to Swift's feud with Kim Kardashian.

very loudly." The backlash made Swift realize that she needed to make some changes in her life. While *Reputation* was seen as a response to the public controversies that had surrounded Swift, it also marked a new era of self-awareness and resilience. It became one of the best-selling albums of 2017.

A Record-Breaking Stadium Tour

In May 2018 Swift launched the *Reputation* Stadium Tour. The concert tour was an elaborate theatrical production that featured pyrotechnics, multiple stage sets, and massive LED screens. It even included a giant inflatable snake, which many believe was a reference to Swift being called a snake by Kim Kardashian. Swift addressed the 30-foot (9.1 m) snake on the tour's opening night in Glendale, Arizona. She told the crowd, "A couple of years ago, someone called me a snake on social media and it caught on. And then a lot of people called me a lot of things on social media. And I went through some really low times for a while because of it. . . . And I think something that came out of it that was good is that I learned a really important lesson . . . you shouldn't care so much if you feel misunderstood by a lot of people who don't know you, as long as you feel understood by the people who do know you, the people who will show up for you, the people who see you as a human being."

The *Reputation* Tour received rave reviews for its visual spectacle and Swift's commanding performance style. It became one of the most successful tours in music history and brought in over $345 million. It set a record as the highest-grossing North American tour as of 2018.

5

Positive Energy

After the darker, more intense tone of *Reputation*, Swift entered a new phase of her career with the release of her seventh studio album, *Lover*, in August 2019. During the *Reputation* Tour, Swift had a realization. She had withdrawn from the public because of the unflattering persona the media and internet had built of her. But connecting with fans on her tour helped Swift see that not everyone accepted that negative version of herself.

New Music, New Beginning

After the tour ended, Swift poured the positive emotions she felt into new music. Ultimately, Swift penned eighteen songs for the album. She recorded *Lover* in less than three months.

The result was an album that was drastically different from *Reputation*. With *Lover* Swift embraced themes of love, hope, and growth. She replaced *Reputation*'s snakes with *Lover*'s butterflies. *Reputation*'s dark colors lightened

Swift greets fans during a promotional stop for her new album, *Lover*, in 2019.

into *Lover*'s pastel pinks, blues, and purples. For Swift *Lover* became one of her favorite albums. "There are so many ways in which this album feels like a new beginning," she told *Vogue*. "This album is really a love letter to love, in all of its maddening, passionate, exciting, enchanting, horrific, tragic, wonderful glory."

The album's lead single, "ME!" was released in May 2019. The upbeat pop song featured Brendon Urie from the band Panic! at the Disco. "ME!" reached number two on the *Billboard* Hot 100 chart.

Lover debuted at number one on the *Billboard* 200 and became Swift's sixth consecutive number one album. It earned 867,000 equivalent album units, a measure of physical sales, song downloads, and streaming sales, in its opening week. It was the biggest single week for any album by any artist since *Reputation*. Lover was Swift's first album to be available to stream in its first week across all streaming services. It had the second-highest streaming week for a pop album, beaten only by Ariana Grande's *Thank U, Next*. Lover was one of the best-selling albums of 2019. It was nominated for several awards, including a Best Pop Vocal Album Grammy.

Split with Big Machine Records

Lover was also notable because it was Swift's first album without Big Machine Records. After more than a decade and after six albums, Swift and Big Machine Records decided to part ways. In November 2018 Swift announced that she had signed a multiyear, multi-album deal with Universal Music Group. She would be working with its subsidiary, Republic Records. Home to other prominent artists, including Ariana Grande, Post Malone, and The Weeknd, Republic is one of the most successful labels in the music industry.

Under the agreement with Universal Music, Swift would own the master recordings for any music she created with the label. The new agreement also addressed streaming services. In the past Swift disagreed with streaming services such as Spotify and Apple Music over the royalties artists received. In 2014 she even temporarily pulled her music from streaming services. In her contract with Universal, the label agreed that if it sold its equity in the music streaming service Spotify,

Swift performs in Shanghai, China, in 2019 amid her dispute with her former record label, Big Machine Records.

the proceeds would be distributed to Universal's artists, including Swift.

Political and Social Engagement in *Lover*

Lover was one of Swift's most socially and politically engaged works up to that point. In the past Swift was criticized for not being vocal about social and political issues. In a *Vogue* interview, Swift recounted a conversation with friend and singer Todrick Hall that left her feeling that she needed to be more vocal in supporting the LGBTQIA+ community. Hall had asked her what she would do if her son were gay. "The fact that he had to ask me . . . shocked me and made me realize that I had not made my position clear enough or loud enough," she said in *Vogue*. "If he was thinking that, I can't imagine what my fans in the LGBTQ community might be thinking. It was kind of devastating to realize that I hadn't been publicly clear about that."

The song "You Need to Calm Down" on *Lover* celebrated pride and equality. Swift sang, "You just need to take several seats and then try to restore the peace / And control your urges to scream about the people you hate / 'Cause shade never made anybody less gay." Swift also introduced a petition in June 2019 supporting the federal Equality Act. The proposed legislation aimed to amend the Civil Rights Act to ban discrimination based on sexual orientation and gender identity. Swift publicly posted a letter to Tennessee's Senator Lamar Alexander urging him to support the Equality Act. "You Need to Calm Down" became an anthem for Pride Month and earned praise for its inclusive message.

Since then Swift has continued speaking on issues such as LGBTQIA+ rights and women's rights. She has spoken

"Soon You'll Get Better"

Swift has a close relationship with her parents, Andrea and Scott Swift. In 2019 she revealed that both had dealt with cancer and her mother was fighting a relapse. Swift documented her powerful emotions about Andrea's health in "Soon You'll Get Better" on *Lover.* The song reveals personal details about how Swift had dealt with her mother's serious illness. She has said that the song is one of the hardest she's ever written because it was so emotional. Swift performed the song for the first time in 2020 during the One World: Together at Home charity concert for health workers during the coronavirus pandemic.

Swift's parents, Scott and Andrea, have been by their daughter's side throughout her career.

Swift poses for a picture with friend Todrick Hall. Hall is singer, rapper, and choreographer.

out against sexism in the music industry. Swift has also encouraged fans to vote and engage with the political process. An Instagram post from Swift in 2023 led to more than thirty-five thousand new voter registrations.

Though Swift had planned an international tour to promote *Lover*, the COVID-19 pandemic in 2020 led to the cancellation of these events. Despite the setback Swift stayed productive and used the global shutdown as a springboard to reinvent herself again.

6

Exploring Musical Styles

In 2020 the coronavirus pandemic swept across the world. To prevent the spread of the virus, many countries imposed lockdowns that restricted people's movements and shuttered businesses and schools. Swift's *Lover* Tour was canceled, as were most of her plans for 2020. But Swift stayed busy exploring new musical styles.

Quarantine Creativity

Quarantined at home in Los Angeles, Swift watched many movies and devoured different types of storytelling. Swift began writing and experimenting with storytelling. "It was really, really freeing to be able to just be inspired by worlds created by the films you watch or books you've read or places you've dreamed of or people that you've wondered about, not just being inspired by your own experience," she told *Entertainment Weekly*.

(*Left to right*) Aaron Dessner, Swift, and Jack Antonoff pose for a photo at the 63rd Annual Grammy Awards at the Los Angeles Convention Center. The trio are long-time musical collaborators who worked together on several Swift albums, including *Folklore* and *Evermore*.

Making an album during a pandemic differed from Swift's previous works. Typically the process is very collaborative, with many people involved. Swift would often be in the same room as cowriters and producers for previous albums. She would test out new songs on friends and band members. This time, however, was much different. Swift worked from a studio in her Los Angeles home. She had video calls with long-time collaborators Jack Antonoff and Aaron Dessner from the indie-rock band The National to produce the album. The typical hair, makeup, and wardrobe sessions were unavailable for album art. Instead Swift ordered several nightgowns online and did her hair and makeup. She and a photographer friend took pictures in the woods behind another friend's house.

Folklore: A Surprise Album

Swift managed to keep news of the new album under wraps until her surprise announcement in July 2020. On Twitter Swift announced that *Folklore* would be released at midnight. She wrote about her experience making the album. "Most of the things I had planned this summer didn't end up happening, but there is something I hadn't planned on that DID happen," Swift wrote. "And that thing is my 8th studio album, *Folklore*. Surprise! Tonight at midnight I'll be releasing my entire brand new album of songs I've poured all of my whims, dreams, fears, and musings into."

> **"Tonight at midnight I'll be releasing my entire brand new album of songs I've poured all of my whims, dreams, fears, and musing into."**
>
> *—Taylor Swift, July 2020*

Folklore was another turning point in Swift's career. The album was a deeply reflective and story-driven work with minimal production. The bright pop tracks of *Lover* were replaced with quieter songs that leaned toward indie-folk and alternative music. Additionally *Folklore*'s songs were less about Swift's personal life and more driven by storytelling with fictional people and places she created.

Folklore was a commercial and critical success. It debuted at number one on the *Billboard* 200 and was the first album to sell one million copies in 2020. The album received widespread praise for its songwriting. "At its best, *Folklore* asserts something that has been true from the start of Swift's career: Her biggest strength is her storytelling, her well-honed songwriting craft meeting the vivid whimsy of her imagination; the music these stories are set to is subject to change, so long as it can be rooted in these traditions," wrote Jill Mapes for *Pitchfork*. In 2021 *Folklore* won the Grammy award for Album of the Year, making Swift the first female artist to win Album of the Year three times.

Evermore: A Sister Album

Five months later Swift shocked the music world again. She dropped a second pandemic album, *Evermore*, in December

Marjorie

The song "Marjorie" on *Evermore* is a tribute to Swift's late maternal grandmother, an opera singer. Marjorie Finlay inspired Swift to follow her musical dreams before passing away in 2003. When Swift described the song, she explained that Finlay still visits her in her dreams. At the end of the song, Finlay's voice sings with Swift. In the music video, home videos feature Finlay sitting with a toddler Swift on a piano bench and showing her granddaughter where to put her hands on the keys.

(*Left to right*) Swift, Antonoff, and Dessner celebrate at the 2021 Grammy Awards. Swift's *Folklore* took home the coveted Album of the Year award.

2020. Swift described *Evermore* as a sister record to *Folklore* and confessed that she could not stop writing songs after *Folklore*.

On *Evermore* Swift worked again with *Folklore*'s creative team, producer Jack Antonoff and The National's Aaron Dessner, and Bon Iver's Justin Vernon. *Evermore* continued with *Folklore*'s storytelling and indie-folk vibe. This time, however, the team felt free to experiment more. Swift and

William Bowery

On *Folklore* and *Evermore*, Swift listed a new collaborator, William Bowery. Bowery cowrote songs such as "Exile," "Betty," "Champagne Problems," "Coney Island," and "Evermore." Fans suspected and Swift later confirmed that William Bowery was actually her longtime boyfriend, British actor Joe Alwyn. Swift and Alwyn met in 2016 and began a six-year relationship. The couple was notoriously private about their relationship and frequently stayed out of the public eye. However the relationship did not last, and the couple's breakup was announced in April 2023. The breakup would become the subject of Swift's 2024 album, *The Tortured Poets Department*.

Joe Alwyn appeared in fourteen films between 2016 and 2024. Swift's albums remain his only music credits.

her creative team did much of the album's work remotely, just as they did on *Folklore*.

Evermore debuted at number one on the *Billboard* 200 in December 2020. It was Swift's second album that year at the top of the chart. Songs such as "Willow" and "Champagne Problems" were fan favorites. "No doubt Swift is still the master of writing a spiteful kiss-off, but the songs of *Evermore* are a welcomed step in a more mature direction, the result of months and months of her getting lost in the woods and questioning her way forward," wrote Shaffer in *Rolling Stone*.

Folklore and *Evermore* allowed Swift to reinvent herself artistically once again. In these albums she explored her songwriting skills and experimented with new ways of storytelling. She embraced new genres and sounds, often to the delight of critics and fans.

7

Taylor's Version

When Swift's contract with Big Machine Records ended in 2018, she left the label to sign a new deal with Universal Records. Under her new contract, Swift would own the masters for her recordings with Universal Records. A master is the final recording of a song from which all copies are made. As the owner of the masters, Swift would be free to use her songs in advertisements, television and movies, future albums, video games, and more.

This provision was not included in Swift's original contract signed in 2005 with Big Machine Records. As a result the master recordings for her first six albums, from *Taylor Swift* (2006) to *Reputation* (2017), belonged to the label. Swift claimed she repeatedly tried to buy her masters from Big Machine Records but was unable to come to an agreement with the label.

Scooter Braun is a well-known celebrity manager with a client list that includes Kanye West and Justin Bieber.

Sold to Scooter Braun

In June 2019 Big Machine Records and all its recorded music assets, including Swift's masters, were sold to Ithaca Holdings LLC, a company owned by celebrity manager Scooter Braun. Swift was devastated. One of Braun's celebrity clients was Kanye West, and Swift blamed Braun for having a role in her feud with West.

Swift maintained that she was never given the chance to buy her masters outright and had talked to Big Machine repeatedly about it. Scott Borchetta at Big Machine disputed Swift's claims, saying that the label had given her the opportunity to earn ownership of her masters in exchange for signing a new contract with Big Machine for ten more years. The dispute sparked debate about artists' rights in the music industry. Well-known celebrities took sides, with Justin Bieber and Demi Lovato backing Borchetta and Braun, while Halsey and Cara Delevingne posted support for Swift on social media.

Charitable Causes

Throughout her career Taylor Swift has supported many charitable causes. She has donated to charities and helped struggling individuals. She has donated to animal shelters and food banks, given one hundred thousand dollar bonuses to her employees, donated to an aspiring student's college fund, and much more. In December 2023 Swift donated one million dollars to the Community Foundation of Middle Tennessee to help rebuild communities and restore lives after deadly tornadoes swept through the state.

Swift launches a Taylor's Version project to re-release all of her original albums. For each Taylor's Version album, Swift re-recorded the album's songs, added new tracks, and updated the album art.

Braun later spoke about buying Swift's back catalog in an NPR podcast in 2022. He explained that he had assumed Swift had decided not to buy her masters before he purchased them. Braun later sold Swift's master recordings to Shamrock Holdings, a private equity company, in 2020.

Rerecording to Regain Control

Pop superstar Kelly Clarkson offered Swift another idea to regain control of her music. "[You] should go in & re-record all the songs that [you] don't own the masters on exactly how [you] did them but put brand new art & some kind of incentive so fans will no longer buy the old versions. I'd buy

Songs and Pens

Swift has written hundreds of songs throughout her career. In 2022 she confessed a secret to fans. She classifies each song into one of three categories: Glitter Gel Pen, Quill Pen, or Fountain Pen. A song's pen category is based on what type of pen Swift imagines in her hand as she writes the lyrics. Most of Swift's songs fall into the poetic and personal Fountain Pen category, including "All Too Well" and "Champagne Problems." A few are Quill Pen songs with old-fashioned lyrics such as "Willow." Upbeat, dance party songs such as "Shake It Off" are written with a Glitter Gel Pen.

Swift dons a colorful costume for a 2019 performance at iHeart Radio Wango Tango in Carson, California.

Kelly Clarkson encouraged Swift to rerecord her early work.

all of the new versions just to prove a point," Clarkson wrote on Twitter to Swift. In August 2019 Swift announced that she planned to follow Clarkson's advice and rerecord her music. By rerecording her songs, Swift would create new masters that she owned, giving her control over licensing her music.

Swift released her first rerecorded album, *Fearless (Taylor's Version)*, in April 2021. Each of her rerecorded albums included all of the songs from the original album and had updated cover art photos of Swift. There were subtle differences in the songs, such as a change in vocal inflection or a slight change in lyrics.

The rerecorded albums also included bonus tracks not on the original album. The bonus tracks were marked "From the Vault." The vault tracks were written for the original album but did not make the final version. They were released for the first time as part of the Taylor's Version rerecordings.

Swift's rerecordings were a massive success. *Fearless (Taylor's Version)* debuted at number one on the *Billboard* 200 chart. Next Swift released *Red (Taylor's Version)* in November 2021, and it debuted at the top of the chart. She continued releasing her rerecordings with *Speak Now (Taylor's Version)* in July 2023. When the rerecording became Swift's twelfth number one album, Swift surpassed the legendary Barbra Streisand for the most chart-topping albums for female artists.

In October 2023 Swift released *1989 (Taylor's Version)*. Not only did the album debut at number one, but it also sold more units in its opening week than the original *1989* did in 2014.

Swift accepts her fourth Album of the Year Grammy for *Midnights* at the 2024 Grammy Awards.

As of September 2024, Swift had two albums remaining to complete her rerecording projects, *Reputation* and *Taylor Swift*.

A *Midnights* Surprise

Amid her masters controversy, Swift surprised fans with her tenth studio album, *Midnights*, in October 2022. Swift returned to her pop roots and her more personal songwriting with this album. The album's theme centered on sleepless nights and the racing thoughts, fear, and memories that can keep one awake at night.

In her album announcement, Swift described the album as "the stories of thirteen sleepless nights scattered throughout my life." She also wrote, "This is a collection of music written in the middle of the night, a journey through terrors and sweet dreams. The floors we pace and the demons we face. For all of us who have tossed and turned and decided to keep the lanterns lit and go searching—hoping that just maybe, when the clock strikes twelve . . . we'll meet ourselves." Hours after the album's release, Swift surprised fans again. She dropped seven additional songs and renamed the album *Midnights (3am Edition)*.

Midnights was a commercial and critical success. The album's lead single, "Anti-Hero," was an instant hit and peaked at number one on the *Billboard* Hot 100. *Midnights* debuted at number one on the *Billboard* 200 and broke multiple streaming and sales records. Critics praised Swift for her mature songwriting and lyrics.

The Eras Tour

If *Midnights* announced Swift's return to pop, the Eras Tour was her triumphant return to the concert stage. In November 2022 Swift announced her new stadium tour and described it on social media as a "journey through the musical eras of my career (past and present!)."

Ticketmaster Meltdown

Swifties exploded with excitement. The Eras Tour would be Swift's first concert tour since her *Reputation* Tour in 2018. Fans were encouraged to register in advance with Ticketmaster as part of a Verified Fan Program to get access to a November 15 presale. Fan excitement quickly turned to despair when they tried to buy tickets. Fans reported presale codes not working, website crashes, long wait times, and other technical difficulties with the Ticketmaster site.

A few days later, Ticketmaster canceled the general ticket sale. The company blamed historically high demands on ticketing systems, bot attacks, and not enough remaining tickets to meet a general public sale. Swift spoke out about the ticketing meltdown and assured fans that her team was investigating what happened and how to prevent it in the future.

Travel Through Swift's Eras

The Eras Tour kicked off in Glendale, Arizona, in March 2023. Over three hours and fifteen minutes, Swift took fans on a memorable ride through her career. At each concert she performed a list of forty-four songs that were her greatest hits and fan favorites. The concert was organized into sections, or eras, each representing a distinct period in Swift's musical career. Swift took her audience through a time machine as she performed her songs. From *Taylor Swift* to *Midnights*, the Eras Tour followed Swift's musical evolution

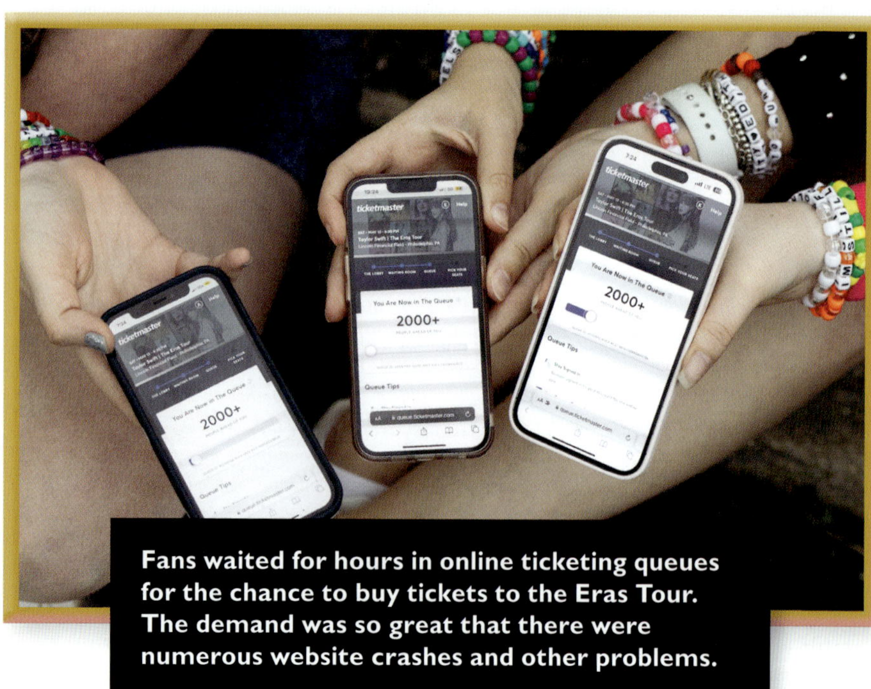

Fans waited for hours in online ticketing queues for the chance to buy tickets to the Eras Tour. The demand was so great that there were numerous website crashes and other problems.

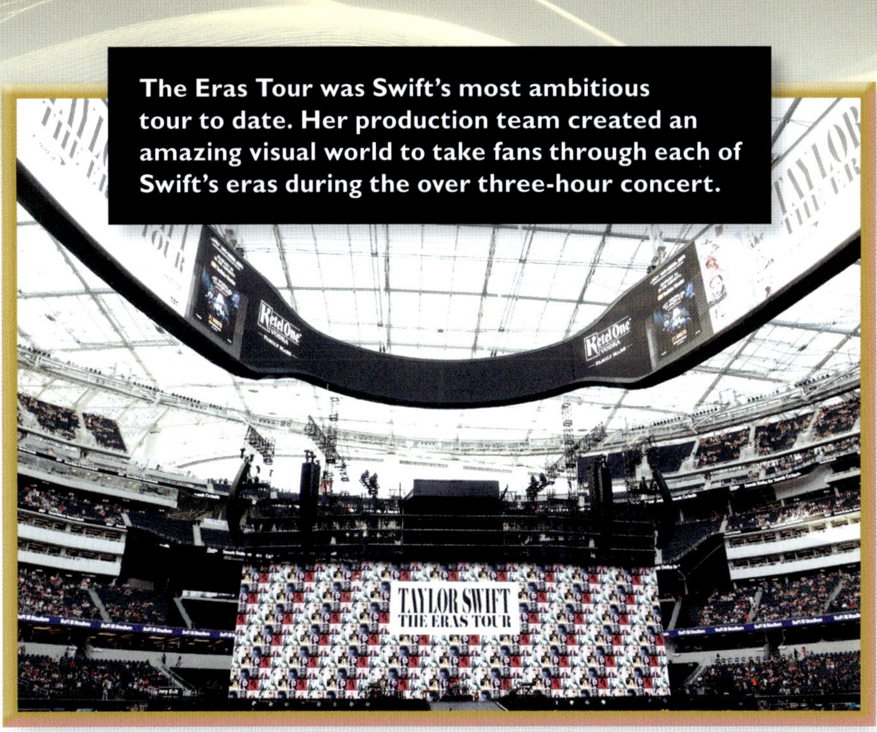

The Eras Tour was Swift's most ambitious tour to date. Her production team created an amazing visual world to take fans through each of Swift's eras during the over three-hour concert.

from country artist to pop and indie folk.

The production design created a visual world for the audience. Each era had its own set, lighting, and costumes that matched its mood. For example the *Lover* era had a dreamy, pastel theme, while the *Reputation* era was darker, with Swift dressed in a black-and-red one-legged jumpsuit with a snake design. The concert used large LED screens, pyrotechnics, and video to move from era to era. The tour's dancers, choreography, band, and backup singers added to the visually stunning performance.

Throughout the show Swift interacted with her audience to their delight. She shared personal stories and made playful comments. Each night Swift surprised fans with two songs—one on guitar and one on piano—that were not on the setlist.

While the concert played inside the venue, thousands of fans who did not have tickets came outside to listen to the

Swift changed costumes around sixteen times during every show in the Eras Tour. By the time the tour ended, she had worn almost one hundred different outfits.

Swift performs in a dress decorated with written lines of poetry on the Eras Tour. In 2024 Swift added a new era to her shows after the release of *The Tortured Poets Department* album.

music and dance with other fans. Thousands more went online to watch live streams from fans who made it inside.

By the end of 2023, the Eras Tour earned more than one billion dollars. It was the highest-grossing concert tour of all time and was less than halfway through its scheduled dates. Every city that hosted a concert date experienced a significant economic boost from fans coming into town for the show and spending money at hotels, restaurants, and other sites. The tour was scheduled to end by December 2024 after a massive 152 Eras shows in fifty-four cities worldwide.

In addition to the live shows, Swift released a record-breaking concert film in October 2023. The film grossed over $261 million globally at the box office through March 2024.

Extended versions of the concert film were also released for streaming channels.

The Tortured Poets Department

In the middle of her global sold-out Eras Tour, Swift took a break to attend the 2024 Grammy Awards. She won her thirteenth Grammy for Best Pop Vocal Album for *Midnights*. As she accepted the award, Swift surprised fans again and announced her eleventh studio album, *The Tortured Poets Department*. Swift teased fans that the album was about heartbreak, and fans speculated that many of the songs would be inspired by Swift's breakup with actor Joe Alwyn in April 2023 after their six-year relationship. Even the album's name was linked to Alwyn, who once talked in an interview about having a group chat with friends called "The Tortured Man Club."

Hours after the album's release, Swift surprised fans again by releasing an additional fifteen songs for a total of thirty-one new songs. Music critics gave the album generally favorable reviews, with some praising Swift's songwriting.

The new album broke several sales records on its release. In its opening week, *The Tortured Poets Department* sold 2.6 million copies. According to *Billboard The Tortured Poets Department* became the most-streamed album of all time and broke several all-time streaming records across platforms. The album debuted at number one on the *Billboard* 200, becoming Swift's fourteenth album to debut at the top of the chart. That achievement tied Swift with Jay-Z for the most number one albums for solo artists. Only The Beatles have more with nineteen number one albums.

Taylor Swift and the NFL

In September 2023 rumors swirled that Taylor Swift had a new boyfriend, the Kansas City Chiefs tight end Travis Kelce. Swift and Kelce confirmed their relationship when Swift publicly showed up to cheer on Kelce at a Kansas City football game. Suddenly Swifties began to tune into the NFL games to catch a glimpse of Swift. The impact was substantial. Social media interest soared. Sales of Chiefs merchandise, especially Kelce jerseys, rose. Swift attended thirteen games during the 2023–2024 regular season and postseason and celebrated the Chiefs' Super Bowl win with Kelce after the game.

Swift and boyfriend Travis Kelce enjoy the afternoon at the 2024 US Open men's tennis final.

Conclusion

Legacy and Impact

Over the past two decades, Taylor Swift has become one of the most successful artists of her generation. Swift began her career in country music but reinvented herself as a pop superstar in a seamless transition from one genre to another. Her albums, from *Fearless* to *1989* to *Folklore*, show her growth and evolution as a singer, songwriter, and storyteller. Her ability to write deeply personal lyrics resonates with millions of fans. Swift's words and melodies have become an integral part of the lives of millions of fans worldwide who have grown up listening to her. Swift's storytelling has also influenced a new generation of musical artists who aim to be authentic and vulnerable in their music.

Taylor Swift has become more than a pop superstar; she has become a powerful cultural force. She has used her global platform to advocate for LGBTQIA+ rights, women's rights, and voter participation. She has stood up for artists' rights

Swift accepts the Video of the Year award for "Fortnight" at the 2024 MTV Video Music Awards.

within the music industry. Worldwide, millions of Swifties have influenced social media trends and driven massive demand for her albums, concert tours, and anything Swift-related.

From karaoke singing to stadium tours, Taylor Swift has accomplished more in her young life than many artists achieve in a lifetime. Along the way, Swift has left her mark on music, pop culture, business, and social issues. She has redefined what it means to be a global icon.

GLOSSARY

amphitheater: a circular or oval building with an open space for performances

choreography: the sequence of steps and movements in a dance or performance

collaborate: to work together to create something

debut: an artist's first album or artistic work

demo: a sample of an artist's music

derogatory: something that is disrespectful

development deal: a contract between an artist and a record label that aims to develop the artist's musical skills

disingenuous: dishonest, not speaking the entire truth

equity: ownership shares in a company

exploit: to take advantage of someone or something for one's own benefit

gravitating: attracted toward a person, place, or thing

label: a company that owns and manages the rights to music recordings

lyrics: the words of a song

masters: the original recordings of a song from which all copies are made

pandemic: the worldwide spread of an infectious disease

paparazzo: a freelance photographer who takes pictures of celebrities to sell

pyrotechnics: a fireworks display

quarantine: keeping people away from others to prevent the spread of disease

showcase: an event where musicians perform for record label executives

spectacle: a visually striking performance

subsidiary: a company owned by another company

synthesizer: an electronic machine that produces music and other sounds

tabloid: a type of newspaper that features gossip and sensational stories

testament: evidence to support a fact

whimsy: playful or fanciful

SOURCE NOTES

6 "New York kind . . . things like that.": Eliza Berman, "Taylor Swift Is NYC's Newest Tourism Ambassador," Time.com, October 27, 2014, https://time.com/3541344/taylor-swift-nyc-ambassador-tourism/.

7 "This album was . . . I was making.": Gary Graff, "Taylor Swift to the Haters: 'If You're Upset That I'm Just Being Myself, I'm Going to Be Myself More'," Billboard.com, October 24, 2014, https://www.Billboard.com/music/pop/taylor-swift-on-new-album-1989-6296366/.

8 "She was always . . . likes to do.": Erica Cohen, "Taylor Swift's Dad Is a Blue Hen," UDaily, September 23, 2009, https://www1.udel.edu/udaily/2010/sep/swift092309.html.

13 "When I picked . . . song about it.": Vanessa Grigoriadis, "The Very Pink, Very Perfect Life of Taylor Swift," *Rolling Stone*, March 5, 2009, https://www.rollingstone.com/music/music-country/the-very-pink-very-perfect-life-of-taylor-swift-107451/.

17 "There was definitely . . . pressure in ourselves.": Jonathan Bernstein, "Taylor Swift's 'Fearless': How She Made Her Pop Breakthrough," *Rolling Stone*, February 11, 2021, https://www.rollingstone.com/music/music-features/taylor-swift-fearless-album-making-1126978/.

20 "In life, you . . . stories and confessions.": Bill Conger, "Taylor Swift Talks About Her Album Speak Now, Her Hits "Mine" And "Speak Now," And Writing Her Songs," Songwriter Universe, October 11, 2010, https://www.songwriteruniverse.com/taylorswift2010.htm.

22 "I look back . . . the core, heartbreak.": Alyssa Bailey, "Taylor Swift Says Red Is Her Only 'True Breakup Album'," *Elle*, October 28, 2020, www.elle.com/culture/celebrities/a34506168/taylor-swift-red-breakup-album/.

26 "Max Martin and . . . pop production styles.": Alan Light, "Billboard Woman of the Year Taylor Swift on Writing Her Own Rules, Not Becoming a Cliche and the Hurdle of Going Pop," *Billboard*, December 5, 2014, www.Billboard.com/music/awards/Billboard-woman-of-the-year-taylor-swift-on-writing-her-6363514/.

27 "He went into . . . them credit for.": Alan Light, "Billboard Woman of the Year Taylor Swift on Writing Her Own Rules, Not Becoming a Cliche and the Hurdle of Going Pop," *Billboard*, December 5, 2014, www.Billboard.com/music/awards/Billboard-woman-of-the-year-taylor-swift-on-writing-her-6363514/.

27 "I was like . . . do with business.": Josh Eells, "The Reinvention of Taylor Swift," *Rolling Stone*, September 8, 2014, https://www.rollingstone.com/music/music-news/the-reinvention-of-taylor-swift-116925/4/.

28 "That song is . . . on the lyrics.": Alan Light, "Billboard Woman of the Year Taylor Swift on Writing Her Own Rules, Not Becoming a Cliche and the Hurdle of Going Pop," *Billboard*, December 5, 2014, www.Billboard.com/music/awards/Billboard-woman-of-the-year-taylor-swift-on-writing-her-6363514/.

34 "I don't like . . . don't like you": "A Complete Timeline of Kimye & Taylor Swift's Feud," *Cosmopolitan*, March 24, 2020, https://www.cosmopolitan.com/uk/entertainment/news/a41965/taylor-swift-kanye-west-feud-timeline/.

35 "They're burning all . . . receipts and reasons": Margaret Abrams, "A Helpful Guide to Everyone Taylor Swift Calls out in 'Reputation,'" *Observer*, November 13, 2017, https://observer.com/2017/11/taylor-swift-reputation-lyrics-mention-kimye-and-joe-alwyn/.

36 "It was so . . . shaking my hand.": Margaret Abrams, "A Helpful Guide to Everyone Taylor Swift Calls out in 'Reputation,'" *Observer*, November 13, 2017, https://observer.com/2017/11/taylor-swift-reputation-lyrics-mention-kimye-and-joe-alwyn/.

36 "A mass public . . . you very loudly.": Abby Aguirre, "Taylor Swift on Sexism, Scrutiny, and Standing Up for Herself," *Vogue*, August 8, 2019, https://www.vogue.com/article/taylor-swift-cover-september-2019?verso=true.

38 "A couple of . . . a human being.": Anna Gaca, "Taylor Swift Talks 'Snakes' and Kim Kardashian at Reputation Tour Opener," *Spin*, May 9, 2018, https://www.spin.com/2018/05/taylor-swift-snake-kim-kardashian-reputation-tour-opener-video/.

40 "There are so . . . tragic, wonderful glory.": Abby Aguirre, "Taylor Swift on Sexism, Scrutiny, and Standing Up for Herself," *Vogue*, August 8, 2019, https://www.vogue.com/article/taylor-swift-cover-september-2019?verso=true.

43 "The fact that . . . clear about that.": Abby Aguirre, "Taylor Swift on Sexism, Scrutiny, and Standing Up for Herself," *Vogue*, August 8, 2019, https://www.vogue.com/article/taylor-swift-cover-september-2019?verso=true.

43 "You just need . . . anybody less gay.": Brittany Spanos, "Taylor Swift Celebrates LGBT Pride on New Song 'You Need to Calm Down,'" *Rolling Stone*, June 14, 2019, https://www.rollingstone.com/music/music-news/taylor-swift-you-need-to-calm-down-new-single-glaad-847898/.

46 "It was really . . . your own experience.": Alex Suskind, "Taylor Swift broke all her rules with Folklore—and gave herself a much-needed escape," *Entertainment Weekly*, December 8, 2020, https://ew.com/music/taylor-swift-entertainers-of-the-year-2020/.

48 "Most of the . . . and musings into.": Taylor Swift, X, July 23, 2020, 7:01 a.m., https://twitter.com/taylorswift13/status/1286270136006184960?s=20.

49 "At its best . . . in these traditions.": Jill Mapes, "Folklore," *Pitchfork*, July 27, 2020, https://pitchfork.com/reviews/albums/taylor-swift-folklore/.

52 "No doubt Swift . . . her way forward.": Claire Shaffer, "Taylor Swift Deepens Her Goth-Folk Vision on the Excellent 'Evermore'," *Rolling Stone*, December 11, 2020, www.rollingstone.com/music/music-album-reviews/taylor-swift-evermore-folklore-1101778/.

56 "[You] should go . . . prove a point.": Caitlin O'Kane, "Taylor Swift Music Rights Battle: Kelly Clarkson Told Taylor Swift to Re-Record All of Her Music Following Scooter Braun Drama. Could That Work?" *CBS News*, July 16, 2019, https://www.cbsnews.com/news/kelly-clarkson-told-taylor-swift-to-re-record-all-of-her-music-following-scooter-braun-drama-could-that-really-work/.

60 "the stories of . . . we'll meet ourselves.": Lauren Huff, "Everything to know about Taylor Swift's Midnights album," *Entertainment Weekly*, October 23, 2022, https://ew.com/music/everything-to-know-taylor-swift-midnights-album/.

SELECTED BIBLIOGRAPHY

Armstrong, Jennifer Keishin. "Why Taylor Swift's 'Fearless' Is Her Best Album." *Billboard*. November 7, 2017. https://www.Billboard.com/music/pop/taylor-swift-fearless-best-album-8029968/.

Eells, Josh. "Cover Story: The Reinvention of Taylor Swift." *Rolling Stone*. September 8, 2014. https://www.rollingstone.com/music/music-news/the-reinvention-of-taylor-swift-116925/3/.

Elliott, Mark. "'1989': How Taylor Swift Shook off Her Past and Hit New Peaks of Artistry." *UDiscover Music*. October 27, 2022. https://www.udiscovermusic.com/stories/1989-taylor-swift-album/.

Ganz, Caryn. "Taylor Swift Announces Second Surprise Quarantine Album, 'Evermore.'" *The New York Times*. December 10. 2020. https://www.nytimes.com/2020/12/10/arts/music/taylor-swift-surprise-album-evermore.html.

Gomez, Dessi. "Taylor Swift's Re-Recordings Explained: What Taylor's Version Is Next?" *TheWrap*. November 1, 2023. https://www.thewrap.com/taylor-swift-taylors-version-albums-explained/.

Lipshutz, Jason. "Billboard Woman of the Decade Taylor Swift: 'I Do Want My Music to Live On.'" *Billboard*. December 11, 2019. https://www.Billboard.com/music/pop/taylor-swift-cover-story-interview-Billboard-women-in-music-2019-8545822/.

Ruggieri, Melissa. "Taylor Swift Rewards Fans with 44 Songs at Eras Tour Opener: Inside Her Triumphant Return." *USA TODAY*. March 20, 2023. https://www.usatoday.com/story/entertainment/music/2023/03/18/taylor-swift-kicks-off-eras-tour-arizona-44-song-set/11490795002/.

"Taylor Swift's 'Fearless' Follow-up Album." *NPR*. December 4, 2008. https://www.npr.org/2008/12/04/97800838/taylor-swifts-fearless-follow-up-album.

"Taylor Swift Moving to Regain Control of Her Catalog by Re-Recording Masters of Prior Songs." *CBS News*. August 22, 2019. https://www.cbsnews.com/news/taylor-swift-moving-to-regain-control-of-her-catalog-by-re-recording-masters-of-prior-songs/.

FURTHER INFORMATION

BOOKS

Bolte, Mari. *Taylor Swift's The Eras Tour Encyclopedia.* Minneapolis: Abdo Reference, 2024.
This book gives readers an in-depth look into everything about the Eras Tour, including setlists, stage design, costumes, and backup dancers.

Klepeis, Alicia Z. *Taylor Swift: Music Industry Leader.* Minneapolis: Abdo Publishing, 2025.
Readers can follow Swift's career in this biography that highlights her skills as a businesswoman in the music industry.

Newkey-Burden, Chas. *Taylor Swift: The Unmissable, Fully Updated 2024 Biography of Pop Superstar Taylor Swift.* London: HarperCollins Publishers, 2024.
This biography of Swift offers fascinating details about Swift's musical evolution and rise to become a global icon.

Perricone, Kathleen. *Taylor Swift Is Life: A Superfan's Guide to All Things We Love About Taylor Swift.* New York: Epic Ink, 2024.
This book provides a biography of Swift's life and career and also discusses each of her albums in detail.

Taylor, Michael Francis. *Taylor Swift the Brightest Star: The Life, Loves and Music of a Global Sensation.* Nottinghamshire, Great Britain: New Haven Publishing, 2024.
This biography of Swift has been updated to include her latest achievements including new music and tours.

WEBSITES

American Music Awards
https://www.theamas.com/
The American Music Awards is an annual awards show, and its website provides information about past and present nominees and winners.

Billboard
https://www.billboard.com/
Billboard's website has the latest news and information about the music industry, including the latest charts.

Country Music Awards
https://cmaawards.com/
The Country Music Awards is an annual awards show for country music, and its website provides information about past and present nominees and winners.

Grammy Awards
https://www.grammy.com/
The Grammy Awards is an annual awards show, and its website provides information about past and present nominees and winners.

Taylor Swift
https://www.taylorswift.com/
The official website for Swift provides the latest news and information about her tours, music, and more.

INDEX

ABOUT THE AUTHOR

Carla Mooney is a graduate of the University of Pennsylvania with a degree in economics. Today, she writes for young people and is the author of many books for young adults and children. Mooney enjoys listening to many genres of music, including Swift's blend of country and pop.

PHOTO ACKNOWLEDGMENTS

Image credits: James Devaney/Wire Image/Getty Images, p. 4; Dimitrios Kambouris/LP5/Getty Images for TAS/Getty Images, p. 6; Rick Diamond/ACMA2013/Getty Images for ACM/Getty Images, p. 9; Jeremy Drey/Media News Group/Reading Eagle via Getty Images/Getty Images, p. 10; Kevin Winter/ACMA/Getty Images for ACMA/Getty Images, p.12; John Mabangalo-Pool/Getty Images, p.14; Stephen Lovekin/WireImage/Getty Images, p.16; Kevork djansezian/Getty Images, p.18; Jason Kempin/Getty Images, p.19; Kevin Mazur/WireImage/Getty Images, p. 21; Cindy Ord/Getty Images for SiriusXM/Getty Images, p. 23; Stefani Chiacchirani '74/Shutterstock, p. 26; Kevin Mazur/WireImage/Getty Images, p. 28; Christopher Polk/Getty Images, p. 32; John Shearer/Getty Images, p. 34; Ian West/PA Images/Getty Images, p. 35; Splash News/Newscom, p. 37; Leah Puttkammer/Getty Images, p. 40; Zhang Hengwei/China News Service/VCG/Getty Images, p. 42; Kevin Mazur/WireImage/Getty Images, p. 44; Bruce Glikas/Getty Images, p. 45; Jay L. Clendenin/Los Angeles Times/Getty Images, p. 47; Kevin Winter/Getty Images for the Recording Academy/Getty Images, p. 50; Dave Benett/Getty Images, p. 51; Michael Tran/Getty Images, p. 54; John Hanson Pye/Shutterstock, p. 56; Kevin Mazur/Getty Images for iHeart Media/Getty Images, p. 57; Kevin Kane/Getty Images for The Rock and Roll Hall of Fame/Getty Images, p. 58; Amy Sussman/Getty Images, p. 59; Rachel Wisniewski/The Washington Post/Getty Images, p. 62; MICHAEL TRAN/AFP/Getty Images, p. 63; Claudio Furlan/LaPresse/ZUMA Press/Newscom, p. 64; MEGA/Newscom, p. 65; Gotham/GC Images/Getty Images, p. 67; Mike Coppola/Getty Images for MTV/Getty Images, p. 69; Design elements: Listiana1979/Shutterstock.

Cover: Imago/Alamy.